PAULIST F

*I*SAAC *H*ECKER

An American Saint

Boniface Hanley, OFM

PAULIST PRESS
New York/Mahwah, NJ

Cover and book design by Lynn Else

Copyright © 2008 by Paulist Press, Inc.

Library of Congress Cataloging-in-Publication Data

Hanley, Boniface.
    Paulist father, Isaac Hecker : an American saint / Boniface Hanley.
      p. cm.
    ISBN 978-0-8091-5232-2 (alk. paper)
    1. Hecker, Isaac Thomas, 1819–1888. 2. Paulist Fathers—United States—Biography. 3. Catholic converts—United States—Biography. 4. Catholic Church—United States—History—19th century. I. Title.
    BX4705.H4H36 2008
    271'.79—dc22
    [B]
    2007049375

Published by Paulist Press
997 Macarthur Boulevard
Mahwah, New Jersey 07430

www.paulistpress.com

Printed and bound in the
United States of America

Missionary to the American People

Throughout his life Isaac [Hecker] diligently worked to promote evangelization in American culture, particularly through the print media. He organized the Catholic Publication Society and became the founder of *The Catholic World* magazine, the director of Catholic Youth, and the author of three books. He did all this while continuing to be the first superior of the Paulists and preaching tirelessly to thousands across the country.

The motivation behind [his] efforts was always the drive to teach everyone the beauty and truth of the Catholic faith. It was the love of this faith that led Isaac Hecker to dedicate his life to serving Christ and Catholic Americans. Today the Paulists, following in the footsteps of their founder (who died in 1888 after a long illness), are present in parishes, campus ministry, major city information centers, publishing, electronic, print, and broadcast media.

Knowing our faith and sharing it with others is the responsibility of every Catholic. Fr. Isaac Hecker is a good example of one who lived out that responsibility.

—From *The United States Catholic Catechism for Adults*

Contents

ISAAC HECKER
A Missionary to North America
Boniface Hanley, OFM

SEARCHING FOR GOD

The orange harvest moon hung over New York City's East River that warm October night. The luminous disk, cutting cleanly into the blue-black sky, released a golden cone of light upon the river's black currents as they raced into the bay below. Sitting alone on a wharf, a young man leaned against a piling, pulled his knees to his chest, and turned his eyes upward to nature's silent grandeur. The gigantic moon floating in the tranquil night bathed his sore spirit.

Seventeen-year-old Isaac Hecker, rapt in contemplation on the East River dock, was experiencing profound loneliness and bewilderment. He had never felt so alone as he did that October evening in the year 1837. For some time, he had inhabited a private world whose features he scarcely understood. From childhood, he believed God had called him to a special mission in life. But now he did not know what God wanted. And, on this October evening, he realized that he had once again failed to discern the divine will.

As clouds cast a veil across the moon's face, now shrunken and pale, Isaac stood up and walked briskly into the city, returning to his work at Hecker's bakery at 56 Rutgers Street. His brothers, John and George, awaited him at the bakery.

THE SON OF IMMIGRANTS

John Jonas Hecker and Caroline Friend, Isaac's German immigrant parents, brought four boys and one girl into the world. The second son died in infancy. Isaac, the Heckers' youngest son, was born December 18, 1819. His blond hair, blue eyes, and high forehead proclaimed his German ancestry. Lively, cheerful, and sincere, the little boy quickly won everyone's affection.

Isaac's father, employed as a metalworker in a foundry and machine shop, helped in the development and installation of an improved boiler for Robert Fulton's *Clermont*, the first steamship to successfully navigate the Hudson River. Later, John Hecker became the owner of a brass-forging business in Lower Manhattan.

In 1822, a yellow-fever epidemic swept through New York City, killing thousands. The Hecker family survived intact, but shortly after the epidemic ceased, Isaac contracted a virulent smallpox. His parents resigned themselves to his death. The brokenhearted Caroline explained to her son the danger he faced. Little Isaac, cheerful and confident, responded, "No, Mother, I shall not die now. God has work for me in this world, and I shall live to do it."

He survived. Until his death more than six decades later, he bore on his face the pockmarks of the cruel disease.

THE METHODISTS

Caroline, a devout Christian, raised her children as Methodists, a denomination that believed God had destined America to be mankind's new Land of Promise. "We believe that God's design in raising up the preachers called Methodists in America was to reform the continent and spread Scripture holiness over these lands," some Methodists proclaimed. Caroline delighted in singing the hymn describing how the faithful would achieve this exalted goal:

Help us to help each other, Lord,
Each other's cross to bear;
Let each his friendly aid afford
And feel his brother's care.

But the Methodists' vision of America was still a dream of the future. The Industrial Revolution's promise of wealth beyond imagination had stoked the nation's fiery energies. Industrialists and entrepreneurs mindlessly exploited America's seemingly inexhaustible resources of people and material. Swelling tides of European immigrants, which began with the Irish and German migrations of the 1830s, provided cheap labor for the mines, forests, fisheries, and factories. Capitalists built huge fortunes, while immigrants were lucky to earn one dollar for a twelve-to-fourteen-hour day.

After finishing grammar school at the age of twelve, Isaac took his first job in the Methodist Book Concern's mailroom. A year later, following the family metalworking tradition, he obtained employment with a type foundry in Manhattan.

In 1834, his brothers, John and George, invited him to join them as a partner in the bakery John had established. John, a shrewd entrepreneur, and George, who inherited his father's mechanical expertise, were laying the foundation of the Hecker Flour Company, which eventually earned them great wealth.

Isaac became the delivery boy and took his first baking lessons. "How hard I used to work, carrying the bread around

George Hecker

Isaac's brothers, George (left) and John, developed the Hecker Flour Company into one of America's leading industrial concerns. John and George Hecker built their first flour mill in 1842 (below). George, the first New Yorker to utilize a floating grain elevator, also founded the International Grain Elevator Company. He held exclusive grain elevator rights in New York Harbor. John and George Hecker were generous to their brother Isaac.

The Hecker Flour Mill

in my baker's cart!" he remembered in later years. "How often I got stuck in the gutters and in the snow. Sometimes some good soul would give me a lift."

Pushing his cart through the filthy, crime-ridden streets, Isaac witnessed the struggles of thousands of people to survive. Corrupt police brutalized an unruly population; in diseased tenements parents sickened and died, leaving their children orphans and prey to criminals; factory fires swept out of control; plagues and epidemics struck ruthlessly.

North of Washington Square, the bread boy stood in awe at the rows of mansions lining Fifth Avenue. Their proud inhabitants spared no expense for ostentation and comfort. When these people sang, "Help us to help each other, Lord," they knew precisely who those "others" were—and they didn't live south of Washington Square.

All the while Isaac pushed his cart through the streets of New York, the problem of his own destiny preoccupied him. "What does the Lord want of me?" he continued to ask himself. His experience as a delivery boy finally convinced him the Lord was calling him to labor for the rights of the city's exploited immigrants.

The Hecker Flour Boy

The Hecker Flour boy has been familiar to millions of American families for over a hundred years.

THE POLITICIAN

Although he had ceased to practice Methodism in his early teens, Isaac still shared Methodist aspirations for America. His brothers had recently joined the Locofocos, the liberal, equal-rights wing of New York's Democratic Party that was opposed to monopolies, to unbridled capitalist manipulation of the nation's banks, and to immigrant exploitation. A historian of the faction said of its members: "These Methodists of Democracy introduced no new doctrines, no new articles into true creed; they only revised those heaven-born principles which had been so long trodden underfoot of Monopoly." Like the Methodists, Locofocos possessed an infectious optimism. Isaac, both believer and disciple, confidently felt God had called him to serve their cause.

The three Hecker boys poured enormous energy into the political campaign of 1837. They purchased a "hand-powered" printing press, distributed leaflets, publicly challenged the banks, and distributed party literature. "George and I posted handbills until three in the morning," Isaac remembered. "This hour wasn't inconvenient for us since we were bakers."

As Democrats gathered at New York City's Tammany Hall for nominations before the 1837 elections, political hacks in thrall to the city's bankers refused to endorse the Locofoco Committee. The political maneuvering weakened both the traditional Democratic forces and the Locofoco faction in which the Heckers remained steadfast. As this hopeless intra-party battle raged, Isaac, aware of imminent defeat and disgusted at political chicanery, often sat beneath the night sky at the East River wharf. He could not discover his life's mission in either Methodism or politics.

A FATEFUL MEETING

As Isaac Hecker was licking his wounds in New York City, Orestes Brownson, a brilliant Boston philosopher, stormed into America's political arena with a book titled *New Views of Christianity, Society, and the Church*. Brownson argued for an uncompromising application of the Gospel to American life. "I dedicate my efforts," he wrote in his magazine, *Boston Quarterly Review*, "to Christianize democracy and democratize the Church."

Isaac met Brownson following his first New York lecture in 1841. "He was a handsome man," Hecker wrote later, "tall, stately, majestic. On the lecture platform he never used manuscript or notes; his thoughts flowed out spontaneously in good, pure, strong, forcible English." At thirty-eight, Brownson, articulate and formidable, became a favorite of the lecture halls. "His thesis," Isaac reported, "was that Christ was the big Democrat and the Gospel was the true Democratic platform."

Orestes A. Brownson

Orestes A. Brownson, an American philosopher, guided Isaac through the early stages of his arduous search for God. When young Isaac, confused and disheartened, visited Orestes Brownson at his home, Brownson suggested that the youth join the Brook Farm Community in nearby West Roxbury. Through Brownson, Hecker became acquainted with New England's leading intellectual figures, including Bronson Alcott, Ralph Waldo Emerson, and Henry Thoreau, at whose Concord home Isaac studied Latin and Greek.

THE DREAMER

As Isaac entered his twenties, his interior life grew ever more intense. Acutely aware of God's presence within himself and increasingly frustrated at his inability to determine what God wished of him, he became more and more introspective. In an attempt to analyze his inner turmoil, he buried himself in the works of the abstruse German philosophers Fichte, Hegel, and Kant.

Beginning in June 1842, he underwent a series of mystical experiences, very often in his dreams. In May 1843, he wrote about a vision that had come to him ten months previous:

"I saw (I cannot say I dreamt for it was quite different from dreaming…since I was seated on the side of my bed) a beautiful angelic, pure being and myself standing alongside of her, feeling a most heavenly pure joy. And it was as if our bodies were luminous and they gave forth a moonlike light, which I felt sprang from the joy that we experienced. We were unclothed, pure and unconscious of anything but pure love and joy, and I felt as if we had always lived together and that our motions, actions, feelings and thoughts came from one center….Now this vision continually hovers over me….I am charmed by its influence, and I am conscious that, if I should accept anything else, I should lose the life which would be the only existence wherein I could say I live."

Experiences like this distracted Isaac noticeably from his business duties. His absorption in the mystical worried John, leader of the Hecker enterprise, which now boasted a six-bakery chain plus its own flour mill. "He's addling his brain with philosophy," John complained. Isaac could only mumble, "My mind has lost all disposition for business."

Now beginning to doubt the reality of his inner life and fearing insanity, Isaac grew more and more depressed. The family doctor suggested that he involve himself socially, do some manual labor, and get married. But none of these solutions addressed his internal fears. Was God really communicating with him in his dreams and mystical experiences? Or were all these simply figments of his imagination?

THE DROPOUT

In December 1842, Isaac, at Orestes Brownson's suggestion, journeyed to Boston to lay bare his inner heart to him. Brownson, father of eight children, received him warmly. After a few days of dialogue, the great scholar, convinced that Hecker's mystical experiences were real, suggested that he join the cooperative community at Brook Farm outside Boston.

George Ripley, a scholarly and idealistic Unitarian minister, had founded Brook Farm in the spring of 1841 as a place where a community of intelligent and cultivated people could dedicate themselves to an uncompromising search for truth. An impressive array of scholars, writers, artists, intellectuals, farmers, tradesmen, and preachers lived, worked, studied, meditated, and recreated at the Farm. Some of America's outstanding scholars taught formal classes there. So prestigious was the Brook Farm faculty that Harvard University approved its curriculum.

Isaac, following Brownson's recommendation, took up residence at the Farm, where he continued his philosophical studies and also studied classical and modern languages, literature, and music. He practiced his baking skills as well. Standing before the ovens, a baker's cap atop his head, the six-foot, blond-haired Isaac, with his clear blue eyes and oval face studded with pockmarks, made an appealing figure.

"Isaac," a female member of the Brook Farm community remembered, "was not handsome, but earnest, high-minded, truthful." The community dubbed him "Earnest, the Seeker." Vivacious and marriageable Brook Farm females were anxious to assist Ernest find whatever it was he was seeking.

A Mrs. Almira Barlow, separated from her husband and twelve years Isaac's senior, launched a determined campaign to marry him. She told the naïve and innocent youth of her love for him. "Almira," he wrote in his diary, "has come nearer to my heart than any other human being." All of her charms, wiles, and affections, however, could not woo the young New Yorker from the angelic lady of his mystic visions and dreams.

"In youth and in early manhood," Isaac wrote later, "I was preserved from certain sins in a way that was peculiar. I was conscious that God was preserving me innocent with a view to some future providence."

HOME AGAIN

Despite Brook Farm's idyllic surroundings, Isaac made little progress toward the goal of establishing the reality of his inner mystical life. In June 1843, after six months at the Farm, he wrote in his diary, "Living is madness." Then, in the manner of the German philosophers he studied so assiduously, he added: "I am, I am not, are correlative; Christianity and atheism are correlative!" Convinced that work in the New York bakery was not God's work for him, he wrote in his diary, "I want God's living work to do." Everything else he did, he judged, "was the work of the devil."

In July 1843, Hecker joined Fruitlands, another scholarly community near Harvard, Massachusetts. Here he began to accept his mystical life as real and beyond his ability to control. He gave up the struggle to find the work that God wished for him and accepted his inability to discern the Spirit moving within him. "What the Spirit may be is a question I cannot answer; what it leads me to do will be the only evidence of its character. I feel as impersonal as a stranger to it. I ask, 'Who are you?' 'Where are you going to take me?'"

Fruitlands

In 1843, Hecker joined Fruitlands, an experimental community near Harvard, Massachusetts, where the residents lived in houses like this one.

For the first time since the beginning of his mystical experiences, Isaac achieved a measure of peace. "It is useless for me to speculate on my future," he wrote in his diary. "Put dependence on the Spirit which leads me," he commanded himself. "Be faithful to it and work. Leave results to God."

In August 1843, Isaac returned to his anxious family in New York City.

A COURSE AT LAST

Isaac returned to the bakery. His brothers encouraged him to involve himself as a worker in the unsuccessful campaign for the nomination of John C. Calhoun as the Democratic candidate in the 1844 presidential election. Baking and politics, however, distracted him from his life of interior prayer and meditation. He detested the competitiveness permeating the Hecker enterprises. And after his Locofoco experience, he found it difficult to trust politicians.

His brothers, sympathetic to his needs, agreed that, if he worked all morning, he could spend the rest of the working day in study and prayer. Isaac devoted his scholarly efforts to English, German, Latin grammar, and philosophy. He grew confident that the unnamed Spirit that moved within him was the Holy Spirit of God, the same Spirit who animated Christ. His prayers took a clear focus. "O, Lord, I ask in Jesus' Name," he pleaded, "give unto me more and more of thy loving Spirit."

As assurance that his mystical experiences were rooted in God increased, his fear of madness decreased. Yet, he suffered a cruel loneliness. At Brook Farm he had written, "I feel as if life is too much for me. It is inconceivably painful to live. I am totally alone." In desperation, he threw himself into politics and causes for the working class to satisfy his hunger to serve his fellow man. His external activity failed, however, to satisfy the needs of his spirit.

In Boston, the indefatigable Orestes Brownson, combating fellow scholars who rejected organized religion, was writing and lecturing on its role in future society. He described his "Church of the Future" as one that would reconcile Roman Catholicism with Protestantism, faith with reason, the individual with society.

He called institutional religion the only effective means for regenerating society and bringing about the social reforms so sorely needed in America. "No work of reform can be carried on with any prospects of success," he thundered, "till we have recovered the unity and catholicity of the church as an outward, visible institution."

Brownson, who recognized that all spiritual growth arose from the individual's communion with God, also taught that people must *share* their experiences of God with others. Arguing that only God's grace can forge this social communion, he declared that Christ won that grace for us and makes that grace of God available to us in his church. By uniting themselves to the church, men and women share the life of Christ.

Gradually, Brownson surrendered his idea of the "Church of the Future" and investigated Roman Catholicism as the channel of God's grace for both the individual and society.

Hecker corresponded with Brownson regularly. Brownson, overwhelmed with work, answered tardily. When he did write, he encouraged Isaac's growing interest in organized religion. A few months after his return to New York, Isaac wrote Brownson: "The necessity for a medium through which the Spirit can act, that man as man can be no reformer, and that the church is the only institution which has for its object the bettering of men's souls, are clear and important to me."

WHICH CHURCH?

Accepting that God acts through the church and determining to serve the church as a minister, Isaac felt that his long quest to find out what God wished of him was coming to an end. As a minister, he would spend all his energies in the service of souls. Thus he would harmonize his need to serve God with his need to serve others. "Such a peace, calmness and deep-seated strength and confidence," he wrote after making this decision, "I have never before experienced."

He informed his brothers of his plan. John and George were not surprised. Isaac's heart was never in the business world.

Brownson approved his plan to study Greek and Latin at Concord, Massachusetts, under the famous Harvard classical scholar George Bradford.

During the spring of 1844, before leaving for Concord, Isaac tried to discern which Church he should join as a minister. He had narrowed his choices to the Roman Catholic and the Anglican (Episcopal) Church.

He visited the famous Episcopalian minister Reverend Samuel Seabury, rector of the Church of the Annunciation on Thompson Street, New York City. Seabury, candid and gentle, admitted that the Roman Church's discipline and ritual were attractive, but he expressed reservations about papal power and claims of infallibility. Seabury advised Isaac to consider all of his objections to both Churches before making a decision.

Hecker next made an appointment with New York's Bishop John Hughes. He asked the prelate what would be required of him to become a Roman Catholic priest. The question coming from one who wasn't even a Catholic stunned the Irish-born bishop. "Two years after conversion is the earliest you can enter the seminary," he replied. After further conversation, Bishop Hughes told Hecker, "You have inborn Protestant notions of the Church," and lectured him severely on Roman Catholic authority and discipline.

"The Roman Catholic Church," Hecker wrote in his diary, "is not national with us, hence it does not meet our wants, nor does it fully understand and sympathize with the experiences and disposition of our people. It is principally made up of adopted and foreign individuals." Bishop Hughes had squelched Isaac's interest, at least temporarily, in Roman Catholicism.

THE CLASSICIST

By May 1844, Hecker had settled in Concord and was well into his studies. He had rented a room at seventy-five cents a week in Henry Thoreau's home. The room featured a comfortable straw bed, a large table, washstand, bookcase, chairs, two windows facing a street covered with a canopy of trees, and one window shaded with honeysuckle.

Isaac divided his time between study and prayer. He experienced such deep peace and joy during prayer that he resented the time required for study. Feeling study might "quench the flow of life from within," he wrote Brownson that he was going to drop his studies and devote all of his time to prayer.

Brownson responded immediately to this letter. He strongly urged Hecker to continue his studies. "Your cross," he counseled, "is to resist the tendency to mysticism, to sentimental luxury which is really enfeebling your soul and preventing it from attaining to true spiritual blessedness." Then Brownson dropped a bombshell: "I have made up my mind. I will enter the Roman Catholic Church, if she will receive me."

Brownson's letter forced Isaac to reexamine his own thinking on the Roman Catholic Church. Brownson arranged for him to consult Boston's young American-born coadjutor bishop, John Bernard Fitzpatrick. After listening to Hecker's narrative of his search for God's will, Bishop Fitzpatrick expressed his admiration for the young man's fidelity and perseverance. The Boston prelate recognized that Hecker's path to the Church had been long and painful, that Hecker had traveled with no human guide, but only the Spirit of God. "The Catholic Church has infallible and divine authority to lead you," the bishop advised him. "In obeying her, you obey God."

Hecker, moved by the bishop's candor and sincerity, decided to become a Roman Catholic. For Isaac, it was "a serious, sacred, sincere, solemn step" that gave him deep peace and "unreachable quietness."

BAPTISM

Isaac returned to New York, advised his family of his decision, and once more joined the business. John McCloskey, New York's coadjutor bishop, helped him prepare for baptism. The Brooklyn-born prelate discovered that Isaac, after years of study, possessed a profound knowledge of Catholic doctrine. On August 2, 1844, after a few weeks of instruction, Bishop McCloskey baptized him at Old St. Patrick's Cathedral on Mott Street. Isaac wrote, "The Catholic Church is my star, which will lead me to my life, my destiny, my purpose."

Bishop McCloskey, who continued as a spiritual director of the new convert, urged him to continue his Greek and Latin studies in New York City. He sensed Isaac's potential for the priesthood, but refrained from exerting any pressure on him despite the need for priests in the United States. The nation's Catholic population in 1840 numbered 663,000 with only 482 priests. The Diocese of New York, which embraced the entire Empire State as well as northeastern New Jersey, had only 71 priests to serve 80,000 Catholics.

Hecker, desirous of surrendering his life to Christ, felt inadequate for the priesthood. He considered entering a contemplative order in Europe. Bishop McCloskey, convinced that God would in his own time make clear what he willed for Isaac, encouraged the new Catholic to cultivate his spiritual life with daily Mass, silence, meditation, and prudent penitential practices.

Brownson, less inhibited than the bishop, wrote to Hecker, "Stay in America. Be a priest. Be a Dominican. We need American priests as fast as we can get them!" Isaac did not know what to do. He considered the Jesuits, the Dominicans, and the Franciscans, as well as the diocesan clergy. He spent many hours in prayer at the Redemptorist Church of the Holy Redeemer on Third Street. "I am unable to choose," he wrote Brownson. "I can only knock, seek and pray, ask for. God has promised to give me a response to all of these."

God did respond. Father Gabriel Rumpler, pastor of the parish, introduced him to two young American converts, Clarence Walworth and James McMaster. Both, having decided to become Redemptorist priests, were preparing to sail for the order's novitiate in Belgium. The spirit of the two young Americans encouraged Isaac to join the Redemptorists. On July 29, 1845, he advised Bishop Hughes of his decision. Three days later he sailed from New York aboard the steamship *Prince Albert*, bound for Europe.

THE NOVICE

Isaac immediately adapted to life at the Redemptorist novitiate at St. Trond, a little town southeast of Antwerp, Belgium. "The conditions here are perfect," he wrote Brownson. "All my seeking," he told his family, "is now ended." After concluding his novitiate, he continued priestly studies in the Netherlands and in London, England. Bishop Nicholas Wiseman ordained him a Redémptorist priest on October 23, 1849.

THE MISSIONARY

St. Alphonsus Ligouri had founded the Redemptorists in Sicily in 1732 to preach missions to Italy's poorest and most neglected peoples. A mission is a series of sermons and instruction at a parish meant to win over non-Catholics or the unchurched and to revitalize the faithful. Since they travel from parish to parish to convert hearts to the Good News, Redemptorists are considered missionaries. Since that time, the Redemptorist presence had expanded to many other countries.

Hecker began his parish mission career in Liverpool, England, in May 1850, under the direction of the veteran Redemptorist missionary preacher Father Vladimir Petcherine. His long search for God's will had taught him peace and humility, qualities which characterized both his preaching and his administration of the sacrament of penance.

In March 1851, after six years abroad, he returned to New York City as a member of the newly established Redemptorist province. As his ship left quarantine for New York Harbor, his eyes swept along the shoreline of Lower Manhattan. The memories of the joys and sorrows, triumphs and defeats, he had experienced on those wharves and in those streets nearly overwhelmed him.

His Redemptorist brothers met him at dockside; later, he had a reunion with his family. It was evident to the Heckers that Isaac had developed inner self-confidence and outer poise. His anxiety had yielded to tranquility; his inner uncertainty to maturity. His European travel, religious training, and pastoral experience had matured him.

Isaac formed a parish mission team with three confreres: his novitiate classmate Father Clarence Walworth, who was a Connecticut Yankee convert; Father Augustine Hewit; and Irish-born Father John Duffy. The four gave their first mission at St. Joseph's parish in Greenwich Village in April 1851. Within a short time, requests for missions from parishes all over the United States overwhelmed the small team.

Isaac was enthusiastic and articulate in this work. A Schenectady, New York, newspaper commented on "the earnest attention of the Catholic parishioners to Father Hecker's admirable and systematic instructions." If the turnout for a mission was disappointing, Hecker visited homes, personally inviting people to the services until he packed the church. Catholics responded spiritedly to his efforts. At Old St. Patrick's in New York, more than 7,000 went to confession and communion during a mission conducted by him and his confreres. In 1854, the group gave a series of missions in New Orleans and Mobile, Alabama.

Hecker's travels across the nation convinced him that America was destined to become a Catholic land. He felt that, if Catholic spiritual life were deepened across the country, non-Catholics would willingly join the Roman Catholic Church. Thus, his personal mission was to strengthen and encourage the American faithful to lead a full Catholic life. He judged his mission work to be "the continuation of the work of our Divine Redeemer. I can conceive of no life so like the life which our Savior led when upon Earth as that of the Catholic missionary."

His travels brought him to the attention of America's bishops. When the See of Natchez, Mississippi, fell vacant, Isaac was one of three priests nominated for the post. The Holy Father, however, gave the appointment of bishop to Father William Elder, who had earned his doctorate in theology in Rome and was then on the staff of Mount St. Mary's Seminary in Emmitsburg, Maryland.

MISSION TO PROTESTANTS

The success of the Redemptorists excited the curiosity of many Protestants. After three years of parish missions, Isaac's little band reported at least seventy conversions from Protestantism to Roman Catholicism.

Isaac, aware that no systematic effort had been made to attract Protestant interest, wrote a book in 1855 titled *Questions of the Soul*, which was based on his own spiritual journey. In place of the classical defense of Catholicism through logic, he presented Catholicism as a religion that best answered the needs of the heart. Christ came to fill us with life, Isaac argued, and the Catholic Church is the means by which he fulfills his mission.

The Protestant press called the work "a two-penny trumpet" and said: "We have not much fear, notwithstanding the brazen designs of Rome, that the free people of this land will ever be brought under the spiritual despotism which has enthralled the millions of Europe." The Catholic press praised it. "The book of the age!" gushed the St. Louis Catholic paper. Within months, *Questions of the Soul* went through three printings.

Hecker published a second volume, *Aspirations of Nature*, to present Catholicism further as the religion that best satisfies the aspirations of the heart for happiness and the aspirations of the mind for truth.

In the spring of 1856, after concluding a parish mission in Norfolk, Virginia, Isaac and his team scheduled four evenings of talks for Norfolk's Protestants. They turned out in large numbers. A fellow Redemptorist described his talk as "the best lecture he had heard in the United States." As a result of this series, at least four Protestants sought instruction in Roman Catholicism.

Isaac approached the delicate work of preaching Roman Catholicism to Protestant audiences with a gentleness, intelligence, warmth, and candor that won the respect of his listeners. He felt his ability was proof of God's call to labor for the conversion of his non-Catholic fellow Americans. "We must make Yankeedom the Rome of the modern world," he wrote.

AN AMERICAN HOUSE

Some of the American-born Redemptorists now began to talk about establishing a specifically *American* house of the congregation. All nine Redemptorist houses in the United States were German speaking, with the exception of the New Orleans house, which was a mix of German and English. So the idea of founding an American house was neither novel nor unreasonable. Further, the Redemptorists, at the urgent request of the American bishops, had already established several parishes for immigrants in the nation's larger cities.

While parish work was necessary, many American Redemptorists felt it violated the congregation's tradition of doing primarily mission work. On the other hand, an American house would preserve the purity of St. Alphonsus's ideal to preach missions to the neglected and abandoned. An American house would also counteract the claim of the bitterly anti-Catholic, American-nativist movement that the Redemptorists were an immigrant order, laboring to destroy religious freedom in the United States. An English-speaking house, Isaac and his fellow missioners reasoned, would also attract young American vocations.

Redemptorist authorities, nervous with the American spirit of independence, did not encourage the move. Superiors of the congregation never grasped the fact that the Americans were not asking for a house limited to American-born Redemptorists but one for all English-speaking Redemptorists.

Father George Ruland, the German-born Redemptorist Provincial, did not believe he could grant permission for Hecker to visit Rome to present his case for an American house. The Redemptorist General, Father Nicholas Mauron, had recently prohibited Americans from visiting him without his written permission. After consulting the congregation's constitutions himself, Isaac concluded he *could* visit the General, despite Father Mauron's ruling, since his visit was not for personal business and since he would be representing a group rather than himself. Fellow Redemptorists Walworth and Hewit of Hecker's mission team, as well as Redemptorist Father George Deshon, agreed with Hecker and signed a testimonial stating that he represented them. Isaac's brother George paid for the trip. Several American bishops gave Isaac letters supporting the American Redemptorist enterprise.

Father General Mauron, alerted beforehand to Hecker's visit, met him coldly in Rome. Mauron accused him of violating his vow of obedience by making an unauthorized journey and his vow of poverty by spending money without permission. In an official reprimand, Isaac was told: "Your way of acting and thinking is by no means in harmony with the laws and spirit of our religious institute." The General ordered him to appear before himself and his board of consultors. The board agreed that Hecker had acted rashly and presented him with an official expression of disapproval, which concluded with the sentence "We dismiss you from the bosom of the congregation!"

"You condemn me, then, without a hearing?" the astonished Isaac asked. They nodded their agreement. Hecker had been expelled from the Redemptorist congregation.

THE CARDINAL

Isaac, determined to fight the expulsion, remained in Rome. He approached Cardinal Alessandro Barnabò, Prefect of the Propaganda.* The Propaganda was the Congregation of the Roman Curia with supervisory responsibility over the Church in

Cardinal Alessandro Barnabò

After his unfair expulsion from the Redemptorists, Hecker found a sympathetic ear in Cardinal Alessandro Barnabò, Prefect of the Congregation of the Propaganda, which supervised the American Church. Barnabò arranged an interview with Pope Pius IX, who reversed the sentence of expulsion and later approved of Hecker's plan to establish a new, American congregation of priests.

---

* *Propaganda* is the shortened term for *Propaganda Fide*; in English, the "Propagation of the Faith," which was the Vatican congregation that oversaw missionary activity. It was not until the two World Wars that the word *propaganda* came to have the negative meaning we think of today. But because of it, this Vatican branch was renamed the Congregation for the Evangelization of Peoples.

the United States. Cardinal Barnabò, made aware by American bishops of Hecker's outstanding missionary work and personal holiness, arranged an interview for him with Pope Pius IX.

The pontiff, in effect, reversed the sentence of expulsion and annulled the vows of Hecker and his American Redemptorist confreres. During his months in Rome, Isaac determined that the best way to serve the Church in the United States was to establish a congregation of priests that would labor for the conversion of their native land. Pope Pius approved his plan and encouraged him to take the steps necessary for its realization. "To me the future looks bright, hopeful, full of promise," Hecker wrote home, "and I feel confident in God's providence and assured of his grace in our regard.

THE PAULISTS

Returning to America in the spring of 1858, Hecker gathered his American friends—Father Augustine Hewit, Father Francis Baker, and Father George Deshon—to plan the new congregation. Archbishop Hughes cheerfully accepted them into the New York Archdiocese, giving them a parish on 59th street for their headquarters. They called themselves "Missionary Priests of St. Paul the Apostle." The group, popularly known as the Paulists, conducted parish missions and the apostolate to non-Catholics.

Between 1867 and 1869, Isaac directly addressed Protestants from lecture platforms, delivering more than fifty-six lecture series and traveling from Massachusetts to Missouri and back. During one Western tour, he traveled more than 4,500 miles and spoke to more than 30,000 people, two-thirds of whom were non-Catholics.

Father Deshon   Father Hewit

Two of the first Paulists: Augustine Hewit and George Deshon.
Hewit succeeded Hecker and became the community's
second General. Deshon was the third.

Hecker's first biographer, Father Walter Elliot, wrote: "We can never forget how distinctly American was the impression of his personality. We heard the nation's greatest men then living....Father Hecker was so plainly a great man of this type, so evidently an outgrowth of our institutions, that he stamped *American* on every Catholic argument he proposed....Never was a man more Catholic than Father Hecker, simply, calmly, joyfully, entirely Catholic."

Another writer quipped, "He is putting American machinery into the ancient ark and is getting ready to run her by steam."

THE APOSTOLATE OF THE PRESS

In April 1865, Isaac added the written word to his lecture campaign, launching *The Catholic World*, a monthly magazine.

A year later, he founded the Catholic Publication Society (now Paulist Press) for the purpose of disseminating Catholic doctrine on a large scale, primarily for non-Catholics. In 1870, he established *The Young Catholic*, a magazine for young boys and girls.

VATICAN I

In 1869–70, Hecker attended the First Vatican Council as a theologian for Bishop James Gibbons of North Carolina. On the trip, he visited Assisi, home of St. Francis. "Francis touched the chords of feeling and aspiration of the hearts of his time, and organized them for united action," Hecker wrote in his journal.

Returning home in June 1870, the fifty-five-year-old Hecker, full of enthusiasm, looked forward to resuming his American apostolate. But God called him then to a new apostolate, that of physical suffering from chronic leukemia. So rapidly did the disease progress that by 1871, he could not continue his work as Paulist director, pastor, lecturer, and writer. He had great difficulty accepting that God, for whom he was doing such marvelous deeds, would allow him to be cut down midcareer.

When he left for Europe to seek a cure, he told his Paulist brothers: "Look upon me as a dead man….God is trying me severely in soul and body, and I must have the courage to suffer crucifixion." He wandered from one European spa to another, worn in body and sorely tried in spirit. Yet he refused to despair. He struggled to believe that God was as much at work in him now as he was on the lecture platform.

He spent the winter of 1873–74 aboard a boat on the Nile River; the sail benefited him immensely. "This trip," he wrote, "has been in every respect much more to my benefit than my

Hecker on the Nile

The Boat on which
Hecker Traveled

When leukemia first struck, Isaac Hecker underwent a severe trial of depression. "Look upon me," he told his Paulist confreres, "as a dead man....God is trying me in soul and body, and I must have the courage to suffer crucifixion." His two brothers sent him abroad in search of a cure. In late 1873, he began a four-month sail up the Nile in the craft pictured here. Isaac (in pith helmet, top photo) joins his fellow voyagers on the bank of the Nile. Despite chronic leukemia and angina, Isaac accepted his failing health through the strength of his faith. He died in 1888.

most sanguine expectations led me to hope. It seems to me almost like an inspiration."

In 1875, the Paulists at home expressed their strong desire to have Isaac return to their midst. He came back and started to work once more, although on a limited basis. His vision of a Catholic America glowed ever brighter. For thirteen more years, he exerted every ounce of his constantly diminishing strength to bring Christ to the hearts of his fellow Americans.

During these declining years, his horizons broadened to encompass the entire Church, particularly in Europe. Anticlerical governments seriously damaged the prestige of the Roman Catholic Church during the later half of the nineteenth century. At the First Vatican Council, the Church, asserting her rights in the spiritual sphere, issued the dogma of papal infallibility. Following the Council, Hecker wrote a remarkably prophetic essay that described the work of the Holy Spirit in the renewal of both church and state. Hecker's theology foreshadowed by eighty years the Second Vatican Council's same interest in the role of the Holy Spirit in renewal.

Illness brought Hecker to a dark night of the soul. He often felt God had abandoned him; he judged the efforts of his life useless. But, as the terrible blood cancer destroyed his body, his soul found new strength. He turned back the despair; he accepted his lot as God's will for him. The Spirit within him brought him new peace and serenity.

Isaac Hecker died December 22, 1888, at the Paulist House on 59th Street in Manhattan.

THE LEGACY OF ISAAC HECKER

Isaac Hecker was an American through and through. He grew up on the wharves and streets of nineteenth-century New York City. As a boy he attended grammar school on Christie Street, worshipped at the Methodist Church on Forsyth Street, and chased the No. 19 horse-drawn fire engine through the streets of Lower Manhattan. The city, already a world center of trade and commerce, left its mark on him through the vicissitudes of his extraordinarily colorful life and through all his painful struggles to fulfill God's will.

He transformed the competitive spirit that was in the Hecker blood into an adventurous zeal that risked everything for Christ. He treasured his right to cut his own path in life. "I have a life to lead," he wrote. "I am called up to lead it. The influence of others shall not swerve me from it." Such enterprise and determination inspired him to open up new frontiers for Christ, the Church, and the America he loved so deeply.

Hecker believed passionately that American democratic ideals and respect for individual rights and freedom provided a perfect soil for the growth of Roman Catholicism. America, he

Original Paulist Residence

Present Church behind Original Residence

When Archbishop John Hughes gave the Paulists a parish at 59th Street and 9th Avenue, the area was thinly populated. The grounds of the original residence (left) and church were ample enough to permit Isaac to have his own vegetable garden. The city quickly grew up around the residence, and mere decades later, the still-standing St. Paul's Church loomed behind it, as shown in this photo (right) from about 1900. The original residence built by Father Hecker has been replaced by a modern structure.

felt, was a land of *tomorrow*, and tomorrow's America could be a Roman Catholic nation. "'Tis impossible," he once wrote to Henry Thoreau of an enterprise he was considering, "therefore we do it." It was that spirit that made Isaac Hecker a great New Yorker, a visionary American, and, above all, a true priest.

A SEVENTH SAINT

Edward Cardinal Egan, Archbishop of New York

On Friday, October 7 [2006], Very Reverend John Duffy, CSP, president of the Paulist Fathers, and Reverend Paul Robichaud, CSP, a Paulist priest whom I have had the privilege of knowing from his years as rector of the "American Parish" in Rome, came to see me. They wanted to seek my support for a decision of the Paulist Fathers to request that the Holy See declare their founder, Reverend Isaac Thomas Hecker, CSP, a saint.

I told Father Duffy and Father Robichaud that, when I received their letter, I was a bit taken aback. For some reason, I explained, I had always thought that Father Hecker's "cause" had been introduced in Rome many years ago. Whatever of this, I assured my visitors that they could count on me for enthusiastic cooperation in the process of both beatification and canonization.

"It would be a great gift for the Church Universal but also, and especially, for the Archdiocese of New York to have Father Hecker raised to the altars," I told them. "We have six other New Yorkers whose cases are being considered by the Congregation for Saints in Rome; they include Blessed Kateri Tekakwitha, Pierre Toussaint, Rose Hawthorne, Father Felix Varela, Dorothy Day and Cardinal Terence Cooke. Father Hecker would make a splendid seventh. He was a New Yorker through and through; and because of the truly daunting challenges he faced in his life, he will be an inspiration for us all."

———

In 2008, when the Paulist Fathers celebrate the 150th anniversary of their establishment, we will have an opportunity to learn more about their extraordinary founder and, most importantly, about the magnificent work they do for the Lord and his church in New York and across the world. We dare to hope that at that time there might be some encouraging news from Rome about the progress of the case of Reverend Isaac Thomas Hecker, CSP, encouraging news about yet another saintly New Yorker.

Edward Cardinal Egan
Archbishop of New York

THE CANONIZATION PROCESS
Michael Kerrigan, CSP

The following summary describes the steps involved in the canonical procedure for causes of beatification and canonization as set forth in the Apostolic Constitution *Divinus Perfectionis Magister,* promulgated by Pope John Paul II on January 25, 1983.

1. It is necessary to wait at least five years after the death of the candidate whose cause is to be considered.

2. The bishop of the diocese in which the candidate died is responsible for beginning the cause. A *postulator* is a church official who presents a plea for beatification or canonization of a particular candidate. The postulator acts on behalf of a promoter group that has formally requested the bishop to open an investigation into the cause of the candidate. The promoter group may be a diocese, a parish, a religious congregation, or a religious association.

3. The process begins at the diocesan level. The bishop forms a diocesan tribunal to begin consideration of the proposed candidate by investigating the candidate's life and writings for evidence of heroic virtue (the *theological virtues* of faith, hope, and love, and the *cardinal virtues* of prudence, justice, temperance, and fortitude). Documents and information are gathered. At this stage in the process, the candidate may be given the title *Servant of God.*

4. After the diocesan investigation is completed, the documentation is forwarded to the Vatican's *Congregation for the Causes of Saints*. A panel of theologians and cardinals from this Vatican congregation evaluates the candidate's life. When sufficient information and evidence have been obtained, the congregation may recommend to the pope that he make a proclamation of the Servant of God's heroic virtue and declare the candidate *Venerable*, meaning that he or she is a role model of Catholic virtues.

5. The next step, *beatification*, requires a miracle that has resulted from prayers to the candidate and the candidate's subsequent intercession. An official Church investigation is done to evaluate the legitimacy of the miracle. When a miracle has been declared authentic, the candidate is given the title *Blessed*.

6. *Canonization* requires an additional miracle, one that can be attributed to the intercession of the Blessed *after* beatification. The new miracle is evaluated by the same process used for the first miracle. Once the Church confirms the authenticity of the evidence supporting the second miracle, the candidate is canonized and is given the title *Saint*.

A Prayer for the Cause of Father Hecker

Father Isaac Thomas Hecker, CSP
(1819–1888)

Heavenly Father,

You called your servant Isaac Thomas Hecker
to preach the Gospel to the people of North America
and, through his teaching,
to know the peace and the power of your indwelling Spirit.

He walked in the footsteps of Saint Paul the Apostle
and, like Paul, spoke your Word with a zeal for souls
and a burning love for all who came to him in need.

Look upon us this day with compassion and hope.
Hear our prayer.
We ask that through the intercession of Father Hecker,
your servant, you might grant us *[state the request]*.

We ask this in the name of Jesus Christ, Your Son, Our Lord,
who lives and reigns with you and the Holy Spirit.
One God, forever and ever. Amen.

Please report all favors received to:

Office of the Cause of Father Hecker
3015 Fourth Street NE
Washington, DC 20017-1102

www.paulist.org/hecker

Isaac Hecker in the 1880s

WHO ARE THE
PAULIST FATHERS?

- We give the Word of God a voice in pulpits and print, on radio and television, on the Web and the wide screen.
- We share the passion of St. Paul for unity in faith and solidarity in mission among all the baptized in the body of Christ.
- We welcome people of diverse racial and cultural backgrounds in our parishes, city centers, and campus worship-communities.
- We claim Isaac Hecker as our founder, the Holy Spirit as our primary guide, St. Paul as our patron, and the laity as our valued partners in mission.
- We search out those who have no church home, and welcome home those who have been away.
- We build bridges of respect and collaboration with people of other world religions.
- The Gospel we preach calls for all the people of God to be treated with dignity and justice.

We are Paulists.
Missionaries to North America.